Star Wars Laugh Chronicles

Star Wars Special

THIS BOOK BELONGS TO:

____

____

ABOUT KODE SCRIPT

Welcome to Kode Script, a dynamic publishing company dedicated to crafting digital stories with precision.

At Kode Script, we believe in the transformative power of creativity and education. Specializing in a diverse range of publications, from enchanting coloring books that spark imagination to mind-teasing riddles and puzzles for all ages, we cater to children, adults, and senior individuals alike.

Our mission is to seamlessly blend entertainment with learning, providing enriching experiences through meticulously designed content. With a commitment to quality and innovation, Kode Script invites you to embark on a journey where every page tells a story and every puzzle unveils a new adventure.

If you like our books, please provide your positive reviews on Amazon or any other marketplace. your support will motivate us to do better.

 email : info@kodescript.com    www.kodescript.com

Why didn't Luke Skywalker trust the ocean?

It was a little too "forceful."

Why did Yoda become a gardener?

Because he had a green thumb.

What's Darth Vader's favorite dessert?

Dark chocolate mousse.

Why did Han Solo break up with his girlfriend?

She had too much Chewie baggage.

What do you call a Jedi's favorite type of car?

A Toy-Yoda.

Why didn't the Ewok sing karaoke?

It was too shy to bear it.

What's a stormtrooper's favorite store?

The Target — though they can never hit it!

Why did Leia break up with her boyfriend?

Because he was acting a bit "forceful."

What do you call a Sith who loves math?

A Darthmetician.

Why don't Wookiees use GPS?

Because they always follow their instincts.

What's Yoda's favorite exercise?

Do or do not — there is no try-cycling.

Why was Darth Vader so good at video games?

He always "forced" his way to victory.

What's a Jawa's favorite drink?

Root sand cola.

Why didn't the Death Star have good wifi?

Too many "dead zones."

Why did Luke bring a ladder to the cantina?

To reach his "high" hopes.

What's the Emperor's favorite music genre?
Heavy Palpatine-o.

What do you call a Sith Lord who loves sandwiches?
Darth Bun.

Why did Chewbacca become a hairstylist?
He's great with a "comb."

What's a droid's favorite type of bread?
R2-toaster strudels.

Why don't stormtroopers play basketball?
They always miss the shot.

What's a Jedi's favorite kind of joke?
One with a light punchline.

Why did Darth Vader go broke?
He spent all his money on dark-side cookies.

What do you call a Jedi in denial?
Luke-warm.

Why was Yoda such a good teacher?
Because he "forced" knowledge on everyone.

What's a Sith's favorite meal?

Dark side tacos.

Why did Obi-Wan go to the bakery?

To find a "roll" in the Force.

What do you call a stormtrooper who writes poetry?

A miss-guided poet.

Why did Luke fail math class?

He couldn't find the right "force" of numbers.

What's a Wookiee's favorite fruit?

Chew-melon.

Why did Leia get an award?

For her "forceful" leadership.

What's Darth Vader's favorite holiday?
Father's Day.

Why did the droid go to therapy?
It had too many "circuit" issues.

What's a Jawa's favorite dessert?
Tatooine pie.

Why did the Millennium Falcon go to the repair shop?
It was "Falcon" apart.

What's Yoda's least favorite candy?
Do-not Skittles.

Why don't Sith Lords do stand-up comedy?
Because they're always too dark.

What's a stormtrooper's least favorite movie?
"Miss Congeniality."

Why did Darth Vader cross the road?
To get to the dark side.

What's a Jedi's favorite type of drink?
Forceade.

Why did R2-D2 bring a ladder?
To reach new "heights."

What's Leia's favorite type of cheese?
Rebel cheddar.

Why don't Jedi lie?
Because the truth is their ally.

What's Darth Vader's favorite vegetable?

Dark side peas.

Why did Chewbacca fail his driving test?

He couldn't "Wookiee" fast enough.

What do you call a Jedi who loves gardening?

A Force-tilizer.

Why don't Sith Lords play cards?
They hate dealing.

What's Yoda's favorite video game?
ForceCraft.

Why did the stormtrooper fail his exam?
He missed all the "points."

What's a droid's favorite subject in school?
Art2-D2.

Why did Leia start a bakery?
She wanted to make rebel rolls.

Why did Han Solo take his Wookiee to the doctor?
Because he had a bad "Chewie" ache.

What's Darth Vader's favorite play?
Les Misérables — because it's dark and dramatic.

Why did the Ewok avoid the cantina?
Too many shady characters.

What's a stormtrooper's least favorite vegetable?
Missed peas.

Why did the droid take a nap?

It needed to recharge.

What's Luke's favorite brand of milk?

Blue Moo.

Why did Yoda refuse to drive?

Bad "steering" I have.

What's a Sith's favorite mode of transportation?

The dark subway.

Why did Leia win an award for her acting?

Because she was a "Force" to be reckoned with.

What do you call Chewbacca on a rainy day?

A Furr-o-cious storm.

What's a stormtrooper's favorite hobby?

Missing targets at the shooting range.

Why did Luke break up with his girlfriend?

She was too "cling-on."

What's a Jedi's favorite type of soda?

Force-Cola.

Why did the Emperor stop going to
yoga class?
He couldn't handle the inner peace.

What do you call an Ewok who loves
gossip?
A fur-monger.

What's a droid's favorite type of
music?
Heavy metal.

Why did the Death Star fail its inspection?
It had too many "holes."

What's Yoda's favorite drink?
Green tea, it is.

Why don't Sith Lords play hockey?
They hate penalties.

What's Darth Vader's least favorite fruit?
Banana "split."

Why did Han Solo bring a towel to the cantina?
To wipe up all the spills he caused.

What do you call a Wookiee with headphones?
Chew-bopping.

Why did Luke fail art class?

He couldn't draw the line between light and dark.

What's a Jedi's favorite workout?

The Force push-up.

Why don't stormtroopers use blenders?

They're afraid they'll miss the button.

What do you call a Sith with a great
singing voice?
A Darth-vocalist.

Why did Leia start a band?
To make rebel music.

What's Yoda's least favorite weather?
Storm it is.

Why did Chewbacca start a barbershop?

He loved hair-raising experiences.

What's Darth Vader's favorite game?

Hide and seek — but only on the dark side.

Why did the droid go to space camp?

It wanted to explore its outer circuits.

What's a Jedi's favorite color?
Light saber green.

Why don't stormtroopers take up archery?
Because they can't hit the target.

What's a Sith's favorite dessert?
Dark side brownies.

Why did Luke bring a flashlight to the cantina?

To shine a light on the dark side.

What's an Ewok's favorite hobby?

Stick collecting.

Why did the Emperor join the gym?

To stay Palpatine fit.

What's Chewbacca's favorite type of candy?
Furry Taffy.

Why don't Sith Lords eat vegetables?
Because they prefer dark chocolate.

What's a Jedi's favorite kind of fruit?
Force-berries.

Why did the stormtrooper take up painting?

To practice missing strokes.

What's Yoda's favorite instrument?

The green tambourine.

Why did the Death Star become a recluse?

It couldn't handle the "pressure."

What's a Jawa's favorite band?
Sandstorm Symphony.

Why did Han Solo become a comedian?
Because he loved Solo performances.

What's a Jedi's favorite cereal?
Force Flakes.

Why don't Sith Lords use alarm clocks?

They rely on the dark side to wake up.

What's a Wookiee's favorite drink?

Hairy soda.

Why did the stormtrooper go to the optometrist?

Because they couldn't see the point.

What's Luke's favorite vegetable?

Leek Skywalker.

What's Darth Vader's favorite fruit?

Grape-saber.

Why did the stormtrooper bring a ladder?

To try and reach higher accuracy.

What do you call a Jedi who loves baking?

Dough-bi Wan Kenobi.

Why did the Death Star enroll in a yoga class?

To find its inner peace.

What's a Wookiee's favorite holiday?

Chew-mas.

Why don't droids ever lie?
They're programmed to be truthful.

What's Yoda's favorite exercise?
Master yoga, I do.

Why did the Emperor get a pet lizard?
Because it was "force-sensitive."

What's a stormtrooper's favorite video game?

Miss-ion Impossible.

Why did Chewbacca refuse to shave?

Because he likes to let his hair down.

What do you call a Jedi who loves cheese?

Mozzarella Wan Kenobi.

What's Darth Vader's favorite board game?
Dark Chess.

Why don't stormtroopers play hide and seek?
Because they can't find anything.

What's a Sith Lord's least favorite color?
Jedi blue.

Why did Luke go to the gym?

To build his Force strength.

What do you call a droid that loves flowers?

R2-Bouquet.

What's a stormtrooper's favorite weather?

Missing rain.

Why did Yoda bring a backpack to school?

Smart packing, he does.

What's Leia's favorite type of tea?

Rebel grey.

Why did the Death Star go bankrupt?

It spent too much on laser beams.

What's a Jedi's favorite ice cream flavor?
Light-saber lime.

Why did the stormtrooper fail geography?
They couldn't find their way to the point.

What's Chewbacca's favorite game?
Hide and Wookiee.

Why don't Sith Lords eat sweets?

They prefer the bitterness of the dark side.

What's Yoda's favorite car?

A Toy-Yoda Corolla.

Why did the Millennium Falcon need a therapist?

Too much "hyper-space" anxiety.

What's a Jawa's least favorite food?

Sandwiches.

Why did Darth Vader visit the library?

To learn about the Force of knowledge.

What's a Jedi's least favorite holiday?

Dark Friday.

Why did the Emperor start a YouTube channel?
To "stream" his dark powers.

What's R2-D2's favorite restaurant?
Circuit Shake Shack.

Why don't stormtroopers go fishing?
They can't catch anything.

What's a Sith Lord's favorite pet?
A Darth-hound.

Why did Luke become a vegan?
He wanted to avoid "dark meat."

What's a Jedi's favorite sport?
Force field hockey.

Why did Leia become a writer?
She loved crafting rebel tales.

What's Darth Vader's least favorite song?
"Let the Light Shine In."

Why did the droid refuse to dance?
It was out of sync.

What's Yoda's favorite season?

Green spring, it is.

Why did the stormtrooper start a
bakery?

To "miss" the dough.

What's the Death Star's favorite
holiday drink?

Black hole coffee.

Why don't Jedi need flashlights?
They've got light sabers.

What's a Sith's favorite workout?
The Force lunge.

Why did Luke avoid the math exam?
He couldn't calculate the Force.

What's Leia's favorite mode of
transport?
The Rebel-rail.

Why did the Wookiee fail his audition?
His performance was too hairy.

What's a stormtrooper's favorite kind
of music?
Miss-tunes.

Why did Darth Vader quit his job?
He felt too much "pressure."

What's Yoda's favorite snack?
Force-apples.

Why did the stormtrooper refuse to play baseball?
He couldn't handle striking out.

Why did the Millennium Falcon go to therapy?
It had too many space issues.

What's a Sith's favorite movie?
The Dark Knight.

Why did Luke start a band?
He wanted to make Force-ful music.

What's Yoda's favorite side dish?

Mash-ed potatoes, they are.

Why did the stormtrooper get fired?

Because he kept missing his deadlines.

What's Chewbacca's least favorite activity?

Shaving.

Why did R2-D2 refuse to clean?

Because it wasn't in his programming.

What's Darth Vader's favorite kind of dog?

A Sith-hound.

Why don't Ewoks eat fast food?

They prefer home-cooked meals in the forest.

What's a Jedi's favorite card game?

Force Uno.

Why did Han Solo bring a pillow to work?

To nap during hyperspace travel.

What's Yoda's favorite fruit?

Grapes of wisdom.

Why don't stormtroopers use Snapchat?
They can't take a shot.

What's a Wookiee's favorite sport?
Wookiee wrestling.

Why did Leia start an advice column?
She's the princess of good decisions.

What's Darth Vader's favorite app?
Dark Mode Photos.

Why did the Death Star take up knitting?
To patch up its flaws.

What's a Jedi's least favorite job?
Sith removal.

Why did Chewbacca go to art school?
To learn how to sketch fur-tastically.

What's a Jawa's favorite board game?
Sand Settlers.

Why did the Emperor avoid exercise?
He didn't want to lose his dark figure.

What's a droid's favorite dance move?
The robot.

Why did Yoda open a taco stand?
Tacos wise, they are.

What's Leia's favorite accessory?
Rebel bracelets.

Why did the stormtrooper go viral?

Because of his "miss-takes."

What's Darth Vader's least favorite candy?

Jaw-breakers.

Why did Luke join the track team?

To master the Force run.

What's Chewbacca's favorite
instrument?
The sax-a-Wookiee.

Why don't Sith Lords play golf?
They can't stay on the light side.

What's Yoda's favorite game?
Hide and seek, it is.

Why did Han Solo start a blog?

To share his Solo adventures.

What's Leia's favorite dessert?

Rebel pie.

Why did the Death Star go to the doctor?

It was feeling empty inside.

What's a Jedi's favorite ice cream topping?
Force sprinkles.

Why don't Wookiees need jackets?
They have built-in fur coats.

What's a Jawa's least favorite weather?
Sandstorms.

Why did the stormtrooper get counseling?

Because he couldn't deal with all his misses.

What's a Sith's least favorite season?

Spring — too light-hearted.

Why did Yoda become a motivational speaker?

Inspiring, he is.

What's Leia's favorite vacation destination?
The Rebel beaches.

Why did the Emperor start a cooking show?
To teach the dark art of desserts.

What's Darth Vader's favorite hobby?
Star-gazing.

Why don't droids play poker?
They're programmed to fold.

What's Chewbacca's favorite hairstyle?
The Wookiee wave.

Why did Han Solo skip the awards ceremony?
He didn't want to go Solo.

What's Yoda's favorite soup?
Split pea, it is.

Why did Luke go to the library?
To check out Force-filled books.

What's a stormtrooper's least favorite math concept?
Accuracy percentages.

Why did the Death Star join a music group?

To play the bass line of doom.

What's Leia's favorite flower?

Rebel roses.

What's Yoda's favorite salad dressing?

Ranch wise, it is.

Why don't stormtroopers play baseball?
They always strike out.

What's a Wookiee's favorite breakfast?
Chew-rios.

Why did Darth Vader start a fashion line?
Because he's all about the dark look.

What's a Jawa's favorite snack?

Sandwiches.

Why did the Death Star take up acting?

To shine on the big stage.

What's Leia's least favorite game?

Capture the Princess.

Why did Yoda become a chef?
Tasty meals, he creates.

What's Darth Vader's favorite workout?
The Force-lift.

Why don't droids eat popcorn?
It gets stuck in their circuits.

What's a Jedi's favorite time of day?
When the Force is strong.

Why did the Emperor open a gym?
To teach the dark arts of fitness.

What's R2-D2's favorite drink?
Robot root beer.

Why did Luke refuse to watch scary movies?

He didn't want to be tempted by the dark side.

What's Leia's favorite game show?

Wheel of Rebels.

Why did Chewbacca start a podcast?

To let his roar be heard.

What's Yoda's favorite board game?

Monopoly, it is.

Why did Han Solo bring a fan to space?

To cool his Solo style.

What's a Sith Lord's least favorite food?

Anything light and fluffy.

Why did the Death Star fail art school?
It couldn't draw people in.

What's a stormtrooper's favorite animal?
A missed-tiger.

Why did the Jedi bring a ladder to the cantina?
To reach higher levels of wisdom.

What's Leia's favorite kind of book?

A rebel romance.

Why did Chewbacca refuse to play cards?

He couldn't bear to lose.

What's Yoda's favorite subject in school?

Gymnastics — flips, he does.

Why did the stormtrooper bring a map?
To avoid missing his destination.

What's Darth Vader's least favorite game?
The Light Switch Game.

Why don't droids play basketball?
They're afraid of short circuits.

What's Yoda's least favorite fruit?

Sith-berries.

Why did Han Solo win the race?

He went Solo!

What's a Sith's favorite chocolate?

Dark Force fudge.

Why did the Ewoks start a band?
They love making forest music.

What's Leia's least favorite type of cheese?
Imperial cheddar.

Why did Luke open a diner?
To serve Force burgers.

What's a stormtrooper's favorite dessert?
Missed-it pudding.

Why don't Wookiees play soccer?
They can't stop fouling.

What's Darth Vader's favorite app?
DarkChat.

Why did Yoda refuse to get a smartphone?
Too many distractions, there are.

What's Leia's favorite dessert?
Rebel éclairs.

Why did the Death Star go to the spa?
To relax its atmosphere.

What's Chewbacca's least favorite chore?
Sweeping fur.

Why did the stormtrooper start a bakery?
Because they excel at missing the mark — and the flour!

What's Yoda's favorite bedtime story?
"Force Tales for Jedi Younglings."

Why don't Sith Lords use elevators?
They prefer taking the "stairs to darkness."

What's Leia's favorite flower?
Princess lilies.

Why did the Wookiee join the talent show?
To show off its roar-some skills.

What's Darth Vader's least favorite
light bulb?
LED — too bright.

Why did R2-D2 go to school?
To work on his circuitry knowledge.

What's a Jedi's favorite Christmas
tradition?
**Hanging up light sabers as
decorations.**

Why did Yoda never get lost?
Path always clear, it is.

What's a stormtrooper's favorite type of comedy?
Slap-miss-tick.

Why did Chewbacca become a musician?
Because he had great rhythm and growl.

What's Leia's favorite type of jewelry?

Rebel pearls.

Why did Yoda avoid scary movies?

Fear leads to the dark side, it does.

What's a Sith Lord's least favorite holiday?

Christmas — too much light and joy.

Why don't droids take vacations?
They're wired to work.

What's Darth Vader's favorite
instrument?
The dark cello.

Why did Luke open a smoothie bar?
To serve Force-blended drinks.

What's a stormtrooper's least favorite song?

"Hit Me With Your Best Shot."

Why did the Ewok start a blog?

To share forest survival tips.

What's Yoda's favorite pie?

Key lime, it is.

Why don't Sith Lords play tennis?
They hate anything "love-related."

What's a Jedi's favorite holiday drink?
Force cider.

Why did the Death Star host a party?
To bring everyone into its orbit.

What's a Wookiee's favorite type of pasta?

Chew-sagne.

Why did Leia start a cooking show?

To make rebellion recipes.

What's Darth Vader's favorite board game?

Monopoly — because he controls everything.

Why did R2-D2 go to the concert?
To listen to electric music.

What's a stormtrooper's favorite candy?
Missed M&Ms.

Why don't Jedi eat fast food?
Because they like things light and balanced.

What's Leia's favorite breakfast?

Rebel waffles.

Why did the Emperor start a bakery?

To make Palpatine pastries.

What's Yoda's least favorite chore?

Washing clothes, it is.

Why don't Wookiees use razors?
They're naturally hairy-tage-preserving.

What's a Sith's least favorite type of bread?
Light rye.

Why did the stormtrooper join the circus?
To master missing rings in the target show.

What's Leia's favorite snack?

Rebel trail mix.

Why did the Death Star take singing lessons?

To improve its "hollow" voice.

What's a Jedi's least favorite dessert?

Dark chocolate lava cake.

Why did Luke avoid swimming?

He didn't want to lose the "Force flow."

What's a stormtrooper's favorite accessory?

A missed-matched watch.

Why did Yoda open a cafe?

Brewing great, it is.

What's Darth Vader's favorite book?
"The Dark Side Chronicles."

Why don't droids go to the beach?
They short-circuit in the water.

What's Leia's favorite holiday dessert?
Rebel yule logs.

Why did Chewbacca learn how to cook?

To prepare hair-raising meals.

What's a Sith's favorite coffee order?

Dark roast.

Why did the stormtrooper join the basketball team?

To miss every shot.

What's Yoda's favorite season?

Spring, it is — green, like him.

Why did Luke avoid the karaoke night?

He didn't want to "Force" it.

What's a Wookiee's favorite drink?

Chew-lime soda.

Why did the Death Star become a chef?
It loved making destruction-themed dishes.

What's Leia's least favorite fruit?
Dark-side bananas.

Why did Yoda meditate on weekends?
Peaceful balance, he sought.

What's Darth Vader's favorite type of furniture?
Dark ottomans.

Why don't Wookiees play video games?
Their paws get stuck on the buttons.

What's a Jedi's favorite mode of transportation?
Force running shoes.

Why did the Emperor love magic
tricks?

They kept everyone in suspense.

What's Leia's favorite board game?

Rebel Risk.

Why did Chewbacca start a bakery?

To bake "fur-real" cookies.

What's a Sith's least favorite
breakfast?
Sunny-side up eggs.

Why did Yoda open a library?
Books of knowledge, it has.

What's Darth Vader's least favorite
drink?
Light beer.

Why did the stormtrooper join a rock band?

To "miss" the notes with style.

What's Leia's favorite party theme?

Rebellion celebrations.

Why did the Death Star start a blog?

To share the dark secrets of space.

What's a Wookiee's favorite cereal?

Chew-berry crunch.

Why don't Sith Lords wear bright colors?

They'd lose their dark aura.

What's a Jedi's favorite flower?

Force-lilies.

Why did Luke enjoy astronomy?
The stars aligned with his destiny.

What's a stormtrooper's favorite holiday?
April Misses' Day.

Why did the Emperor avoid theme parks?
Too much light-hearted fun.

What's Leia's favorite type of bread?

Rebel baguettes.

Why did Chewbacca take up yoga?

To stay flexibly fierce.

What's a Sith's favorite candy bar?

Dark Snickers.

Why did Yoda become a tour guide?

Paths of wisdom, he shows.

What's Darth Vader's favorite dessert?

Dark fudge brownies.

Why did the Wookiee join a choir?

To hit all the growl notes.

What's a Jedi's favorite yoga pose?

The Force warrior stance.

Why did Leia love puzzles?

Piecing together the rebellion, she does.

Thank
You!